CINDY LEE

Mastering Mortgage Field Inspections

A Guide To Success and Full Time Income

Contents

1

Introduction

Welcome to Mastering Mortgage Field Inspections. My name is Cindy Lee, and I am extremely excited to be sharing with you what I have learned after completing thousands of inspections and training hundreds of inspectors in several different states.

Field inspectors are needed for various reasons, like when a loan becomes delinquent or past due. The mortgage company is required to send someone to the property to take photos and to determine the occupancy status of the property along with its general condition.

I'm also excited because a lot of people don't even know that this side of the business exists. The number of foreclosures is expected to rise in 2024. There are over eighty-four million mortgages in the United States. This represents 72.5 percent of consumer debt.

Most real estate experts don't expect another foreclosure spike like the one during the great recession. A potential uptick in 2024 is expected due to economic factors and market dynamics. New laws and requirements require a mortgage applicant to be more qualified to get a loan today. This has helped to eradicate the riskier loans and lower the foreclosure market. There are now more buyers than homes for sale.

Now some good news. The number of homeowners losing their properties dropped twenty three percent from October and thirty two percent from last year. After all this is said, field inspectors are essential to the health and well-being of the housing market. Therefore, field inspectors are needed across the United States.

This book was written to help anyone looking to get into the industry, whether you want to supplement your income, or you want to create your own business. Many real estate agents, notaries and mortgage officers supplement their incomes when real estate sales are down. Retirees also like to supplement their social security to help keep up with inflation. Single Mom's like to do inspections while their kids are in school. So, the job could be perfect for anyone looking for a flexible schedule. I won't go into a lot of detail in this book as to how you complete each type of inspection. I will talk about the different types of inspections and provide you with valuable information to see if this might be right for you. Although it's not always required, you will have some contact with homeowners while in the field. If you have a big fear of speaking to people and don't like to drive, this may not be for you. If you enjoy working outside, need a flexible schedule, don't mind talking to others and want to work independently, then this might be just the thing you have been looking for.

Let's dive in and explore the exciting world of mortgage field inspections.

2

Chapter 2

T he Mortgage Field Inspection Process

Many homeowners struggle throughout the nation with foreclosures, mostly in the Mid-Atlantic, Ohio, South Carolina, and parts of California. Delaware had the highest percentage of foreclosure filings in November with one in every 2,393 homes at risk. Maryland with one in every 2,537 homes. Ohio with one in every 2,656 homes, South Carolina with one in every 2,711 homes and New Jersey with one in every 2,834 homes. Bakersfield CA had the most foreclosure filings with one in every 1,595 homes. Next was Cleveland with one in every 1,818 homes, Canton OH with one in every 1820 homes, Columbia SC with one in every 1,922 homes and Stockton CA with one in every 1,961 homes. (Only metros with at least 200,000 residents were included in this part of the ATTOM analysis.) Filings include default notices, bank repossessions, and arranged auctions.

When a loan becomes past due, the banks or mortgage companies are required to send a field inspector to the property to take photos and to determine if the property is occupied or vacant. The inspector will also check the condition of the property and document any damage. Field inspectors are independent contractors and are responsible for

3

getting their inspections completed on time. Most inspectors receive 1099's and are responsible for their own taxes. Please consult a tax professional to educate yourself on all possible tax deductions.

Successful field inspectors must have the ability to work responsibly with little supervision and must be efficient in scheduling and routing their inspections. A good work ethic is essential because there is no one physically there to help you complete the inspection. You must be a self-starter and responsible in every aspect. Inspection companies are always looking for reliable, and trustworthy inspectors.

I was in the field for over ten years. I expanded my territory until I was covering six counties and working for two to three companies at a time. When companies see that you are reliable and trustworthy, your services will be in high demand. People might observe you doing inspections and want to also become an inspector. Many think that we just drive around and take pictures, but there is much more to it than that. Although the job is not difficult, it does require attention to detail and each client's requirements. There are usually several different clients with several different requirements. Purchasing cars that get good gas mileage will increase profits. Currently a Kia Niro gets approximately fifty miles to the gallon. That equals approximately five hundred miles to a tank full. This puts more dollars in your pocket instead of the gas tank. The job is easier if you have the right tools. Being organized in the field will create more production and more money. No business was ever built without an investment. The biggest investment is your time and effort. Some companies may require background checks and you might need a little gas money and a few tools to get started. Compared to other businesses, startup costs for this one are minimal.

This would be your business. It's a business that you must build. If one company isn't giving you enough work to sustain you, then reach out to others. Inspections can be done for other companies in the same areas. The lenders hire all kinds of different companies to complete inspections.

There are also phone apps out today that you can download to your phone, sign up and do inspections without going through a big hiring process. If an inspection pops up on your phone and you grab it before someone else, then it is yours. It's first come, first serve. These usually pay instantly after the inspection is approved. These inspections usually must be done the same day, but the pay is higher than some regular inspections.

There are many different types of inspections and getting yourself familiar with them is suggested.

1.)Exterior Inspections- Inspect the exterior condition of the property, including the roof, exterior siding or veneers, windows, doors, and landscaping.
2.)Interior Inspections- Inspect the interior condition of the property including any structural damage including flooring, walls, ceilings, electrical systems, plumbing fixtures, and any personal property left behind.
3.)Occupancy Inspections- Inspect to determine if the property is occupied, vacant or abandoned. These inspections are sometimes completed from the street but may also require you to step on the property. Check for occupancy by testing the utilities or looking for personal property.
4.)Insurance Inspections- Inspect the property's insurability checking for potential risks such as fire hazards, safety issues and to make sure the property is following the insurance company's requirements.
5.)Damage Inspections- Inspect the property after an accident, natural disaster, or other event to assess the damage and determine the extent of the repairs needed and completed for insurance or mortgage purposes.

6.)Pre-Foreclosure Inspection- Inspect properties facing foreclosure to assess their condition, occupancy status and value.

7.)Post-Foreclosure Inspections- Inspect after a property has been foreclosed upon and assess its condition and prepare if for resale.

8.)Draw Inspections- Inspect the property undergoing renovation or new construction to ensure funds are disbursed based on the progress of the repairs.

9.)Specialized Inspections- Inspect specific property types, tailored specifically to a client's needs such as commercial properties, multi-family residences, government owned assets and agricultural properties.

10.) Loan Modification Inspections- These require inspectors to make up to 3 separate attempts trying to contact the homeowners to sign their loan modification paperwork.

11.) Reverse Mortgage Inspections- trying to contact the homeowner to sign a certification that they still occupy the property. Reverse mortgages require the homeowner to live on the property.

You are a representative of the mortgage company and are performing inspections on their behalf. You have a legal right to inspect and access properties, if it doesn't constitute an illegal trespass The Code of Federal Regulations 203.377 states: The mortgagee, upon learning that a property subject to a mortgage is vacant or abandoned shall be responsible for the inspection of such property at least monthly if the loan is in default. When a mortgage is in default and payment is not received within 45 days of the due date and efforts to reach the mortgagor by telephone have been unsuccessful, the mortgagee shall take reasonable action to protect and preserve such property when it has been determined to be abandoned or vacant until its conveyance to the Secretary. When completing no contact occupancy inspections. It is important that the inspector doesn't step or drive onto the property.

Never disclose why you are inspecting a property to anyone because it is a major violation of The Fair Debt Collection Practices Act. It is important to know the legal aspects of the inspection process.

3

Chapter 3

Preparing for the Field

Review assignment instructions and requirements, so that you know what type of inspection you will be completing and what forms you may or may not need. There is nothing worse than driving to a property and then realizing you forgot something and can't complete it. Check your vehicle and make sure all liquids are topped off and there is plenty of air in all your tires. Organize yourself the night before. This will save you time in the field.

It takes about 3 months to become a good inspector. The first month you are learning how to complete the various types of inspections and all the different client's requirements. Month two you will be learning how to route multiple properties to maximize efficiency. On the third month you will combine all your newly acquired skills to become a quicker and more efficient inspector.

Most inspections must be completed in daylight hours. Inspectors love the summertime because you have more daylight to complete inspections. That usually equals more money. Depending on the time of year and where you are located, daylight can last anywhere from 7-16 hours. So, it's pretty much self-explanatory. The more daylight hours that you have, the more time to complete inspections. That means….. more money, more money, more money.

Gather all the necessary tools so that work is completed at a more efficient rate. These may include:

1. A reliable and economical car
2. Computer
3. Smartphone
4. Printer
5. Background check
6. I.D. Badge
7. Blue painter's tape or regular tape
8. Volt stick
9. Folder filing system
10. Bug spray
11. Measuring tape
12. Selfie stick

Not all these items may be needed. It depends on the client that you are working for. All of them have their own stipulations. Make sure to check with anyone you are working for and ask about their company requirements.

Always remain professional and remember that all information provided to you is confidential. The dress code for inspectors is usually business casual but it is suggested that you check with whomever assigns you the inspections. It is suggested that you wear sturdy boots in case of high vegetation, but also carry rain boots for rainy days and in case of standing water.

It is also suggested that you carry an emergency bag. You never know when you might get stuck in traffic, fall in the mud, have mosquitos attacking you, or a low or flat tire, etc. Carry everything you might need if you were stranded for any extended length of time. Nothing may ever happen, but if it does, you will be grateful for that emergency bag.

4

Chapter 4

On Site Inspections

Before arriving at the property, it is recommended to know what type of inspection you are performing.

If the inspection requires that you do not contact the homeowner, then you might want to pull a couple of houses up or a couple of houses down, while filling out your report. Then quickly get out of the vehicle and take the required photos. This way, you can inspect the property without alerting the homeowner. These types of inspections are ordered when a homeowner has filed for bankruptcy. As a representative of the bank, an inspector is not allowed to step on the property for these types of inspections. All photos must be taken from the street or a public right of way. If the homeowner should catch you taking photos and speak to you first, then they are initiating contact. Even if they invite you on to the property say "no" and ask them to come down and speak to you. While speaking to them, inform them that you are there on behalf of their mortgage company and we're asked to verify that the property was occupied. You were also instructed not to bother the homeowner. If they ask why you are taking photos, explain that it's a requirement of their lender to provide photos with your digital report. If you are not able to get all the required photos, it is suggested that you pull away from the property. Get out of your vehicle, zoom in on your camera and get the best pictures you can of the property. If the homeowner is watching you like a hawk, you can't do that. Then you might just have to capture several pictures of the street signs. Sometimes that's all you can do to complete the inspection the first time. If you must go back a second time, you're losing money.

If an inspection requires you to contact the homeowner, it is suggested that you take the photos before knocking on the door. Not that you are trying to be sneaky, but some homeowners get nervous or upset if they see you taking photos. If they don't see you taking pictures, then they can't ask why you are taking pictures. It is perfectly legal to take any photos from the street as long as there are no people in them. If a homeowner becomes hostile and won't allow you to take the required photos, then you must have photos to replace them, even if you must take several pictures of the same thing, or pictures from far away. Just attach the required photo labels to those photos and move on.

When dealing with neighbors, inspectors are required not to reveal to anyone the reason for the inspection. All information is confidential. If a neighbor asks why you are there, you are a property inspector. Never mention to them that you represent the mortgage company, except to the owner of the property you are inspecting. If the owner wants any more information, they need to reach out to the mortgage company. Neighbors can be aggressive. Leave the property if you feel that your safety is an issue.

Never take people's reactions personally. No one knows what others are going through so never engage with a hostile homeowner. Just get back in your car and leave the property. If you ever feel a need, you can call the police if your safety is an issue. If the homeowner calls the police on the inspector, it is suggested that you wait for the police to get there. Stay in your car and pull down the street away from the house.

Stay close enough to see when the police will arrive. You have every legal right to be in the street as well as taking pictures from the street. It is not breaking the law.

Inspectors deal with many different scenarios while in the field. With proper training and know-how, these obstacles can be handled safely and responsibly.

5

Chapter 5

Using Technology in Inspections

Before the invention of cell phones, pictures were taken with cameras. An inspector then had to download them to a computer and upload them onto a website. Inspectors were not able to complete the inspection in real time. Inspections had to be completed at home after you had worked all day. Can you image having to go home after you have worked for 8-10 hours and then still having to work a couple of hours after getting home? How would you like to have to remember all the little details on numerous properties every day, then successfully route your properties manually with a map book or Thomas Guide (I might be aging myself here)? An inspector might have been lucky to cover 20 properties a day doing it that way. Today, an inspector can complete numerous properties in a day thanks to modern day technology.

Technology has streamlined the inspection process by providing tools such as mobile apps to collect the data, location tracking for efficient routing, digital cameras for taking photos and cloud-based platforms for more accurate reporting and communication. Inspections are now completed inside a mobile phone app so the inspection is completed while still at the property. Technology has helped to reduce paperwork, increase productivity, and improve accuracy. Digital technology and satellite imagery are valuable when it comes to properties where on-site inspections are challenging or unfeasible due to remote or hazardous locations.

Digital reporting also provides clarity throughout the inspection process. This allows stakeholders to track the status of inspections immediately and access detailed reports instantaneously.

Automated scheduling systems and other integrated software solutions also help cut down on administrative tasks. This allows the inspector more time on-site and less time on paperwork.

By reducing paperwork and minimizing travel requirements through remote technologies, and digitization helps contribute to environmental sustainability efforts by lowering carbon emissions and reducing paper waste.

There are some clients who will accept inspections done remotely, but very few. Drones and virtual reality may be used in the future for remote inspections. While writing this book, I have yet to see it. That doesn't mean it isn't already being done.

6

Chapter 6

Communication

Communication is a key element in mortgage field inspections. It provides clear and timely communication between inspectors, lenders, and stakeholders. It plays a crucial role in solving any problems or issues that may arise during an inspection.

Contact with property owners, occupants and contractors may be necessary to complete certain types of inspections. They may need to gain access to the property or may need clarification on certain details that are not available. Clear and professional communication is necessary to make sure that all necessary actions are taken, and the inspection process goes smoothly.

In the event of a change in scheduling, or an unexpected delay, prompt communication with clients or stakeholders reduces the risk of any disruptions and ensures that all deadlines are met.

Good communication develops trust and cooperation. This leads to smoother and more successful results. The more trustworthy and reliable you are, the more successful you will be in this industry.

7

Chapter 7

Completing Inspection Reports

Each inspection requires photos and answering a series of questions regarding the property. It is important that your reports are clear and to the point. It requires paying close attention to detail and making sure that the whole report tells the story. Reports are usually multiple-choice questions. How you answer the questions determines what pictures the inspector needs to provide. The photos and the report must match. If they conflict in any way the inspector is sent back to the property. Pay is not issued until the inspector returns to the property and corrects the inspection. This happens when inspectors don't follow instructions, provide enough photos, or miss a required action. It is very important to read and follow the instructions carefully so that the inspection is completed on the first trip. The same houses are usually visited every month. When you fill out the report the second time, some of the answers from last month will already be prepopulated. That means there are not as many questions to answer, which means less time at the property. After completing a few inspections, you will notice that you are more familiar with the questions. I personally got so familiar with the questions that I could answer quickly before I read them.

Inspection reports detail the size, condition, and occupancy of the property as well as any special features or any issues the inspector observes on site. If you cannot see or drive up to the property for any reason, then the report is very short, because an inspector cannot provide the occupancy status of a property if they can't see it. The property might be off a private road, might be completely cut off from public access, or it might be in a gated community.

Depending on the occupancy status of the property the length of the report will vary with the different types of inspections. Many inspections just require exterior reporting but if the property is vacant, then the client will want a more extensive inspection. At a full interior exterior inspection, there will be more questions to answer and more photos to capture. These inspections take longer but they also pay more.

Before submitting your inspection, it is good practice to check it first. Look for any obstacles in the photos like fingers, people, etc. You must exit your vehicle to take photos. Also check to make sure that you have answered everything correctly and at a quick glance, the report is clear and accurate.

The reports will ask for a lot of detail, even when we are just checking the occupancy status. Sometimes you must answer the questions to the best of your ability. The report may ask about property value. If the inspector isn't a real estate agent or appraiser, they may not know this information. All you can do is answer it to the best of your ability. An inspection cannot be completed if all the questions are not answered.

Photos are part of the report as well. As a reminder, never take photos with people in them. Inspections are mainly done during daylight hours. Some inspections are completed at night but very few and are ordered by the client specifically. Make sure that all photos are of the highest quality and that they prove everything that you report. Don't take photos at dusk. Also, watch out when you are taking multiple photos.

It's very easy to get your fingers in a photo. Once it is submitted, it can't be changed or corrected. It's important to check your report and your pictures before submission. If the client finds any mistakes or discrepancies, they can send an inspector back to correct them.

Each client has their own picture requirements. Reading each inspection instruction carefully and answering all the inspection questions first, in some mobile apps, highlights the label of the required photos. It's best practice to always know the picture requirements for each type of inspection for accuracy.

8

Chapter 8

Difficult Conditions and Challenges
Like any other job there are challenges. What if I can't find an address? What if there is no house number? What if the community is gated? What if there is no street sign? What if access is blocked by a weather event? What if there's a squatter in the house? What if you find the property occupied when it's supposed to be vacant? What if the homeowner inquires why you are there? What if they are hostile? What if a homeowner calls the police? What if a neighbor asks what you are doing? How do you handle loose dogs on a property? What if you are given a no contact order and someone is already outside? What if a homeowner doesn't show up for a scheduled inspection? What if the homeowner won't even set the appointment? What do you do if a homeowner asks you not to take photos? These are all things that are learned in time and can be discussed later. Maybe my next book?

Vehicles can break down. A well-maintained vehicle will keep you on the road and making money. If anything is preventing you from getting to a property, take a photo of what is preventing access. An inspector's safety should always be the number one concern.

Speaking of difficult situations and challenges. I also carry a pair of gloves. Why do you ask? I was running a route in Palm Springs CA. The temperature was 110° that day. I was trying to change a flat tire, but everything was so hot I was getting burned every time I touched anything. The street was scalding hot. After that I learned to carry a pair of gloves.

When I first moved from California to Mississippi, I kept getting stuck because California is bedrock, and the ground is hard. Here in Mississippi one tire can touch the grass and sink down one to two inches. It happens before you know it. Lucky for me, there are a lot of southern gentlemen living in Mississippi. Not once did I call a tow truck! A nice gentleman always came by and pulled me out. What a change from California.

Pay close attention when you are driving so that you are not in an accident. Inspectors sometimes have several things going on and it's very easy to take your attention away for just a second. If you're running behind schedule, don't speed or drive recklessly. No inspection is worth getting in an accident. Don't speed through neighborhoods. There are kids playing and the speed limit is usually 25 miles per hour. Inspectors visit the same neighborhoods repeatedly. Things run more smoothly if you don't upset the neighbors.

Always act like you would want someone to act if they came to your house and started taking pictures. Be respectful to everyone. Have respect for their property. If asked to leave, an inspector should not take it personally, and leave the property immediately. Never engage with a hostile homeowner.

Some challenges can be overcome, and some cannot. Just document everything well in the reports and provide photos. Satisfying the client is the top priority. They understand that inspectors are dealing with lots of different elements. Difficult conditions and challenges can be handled professionally when staying calm and in control.

People can be crazy, just watch the news. After 10 years in the field, I've been asked to leave the property. I've been asked not to come back. These types of issues should be documented so that when an inspector returns to the property next month, the notes are available to the inspector such as an aggressive homeowner, dogs on the property, etc. Document any interaction with homeowners or neighbors.

9

Chapter 9

Continue Learning

The industry is ever changing and there are always things to learn. Participate in any continued education classes or training programs. Anything that will help you with personal or professional development should be taken advantage of. If someone gives you feedback on an inspection, they are just trying to help you get it right. When I started, I was provided with no training at all and had to learn things the hard way. This caused a lot of frustration and paralyzed my production and my ability to make money. Push through and learn from your mistakes. The best learning is through mistakes. Learn as much as you can, turn your brain into a sponge. Some inspectors take on multiple territories and train drivers and work under them. Learning how to complete multiple types of inspections brings more opportunities and better money. Find your niche and go for it. Stay updated on any changes in the industry and don't be surprised if sometimes the clients change their requirements. With proper training and the right tools and a positive attitude, anyone can become a successful inspector.

10

Chapter 10

Conclusion

I've been in the mortgage field business for over 10 years. Even though my background was in real estate and ministry. I truly enjoyed the time I was in the field. I was able to meet a lot of great people and not so great people. I was able to see all kinds of houses and a lot of beautiful scenery. I live on the coast so driving down the coastline while working wasn't difficult at all. Due to having melanoma removed from my left forearm, it was time to get out of the field for health reasons.

I lived in California most of my life and have spent the last 11 years in Mississippi. After driving around Mississippi performing inspections for 10 years. I know Mississippi better than I ever knew California.

I now am very passionate about training other drivers. I care about people, and I want to help anyone that is interested in doing this. The struggles I went through I don't wish on anyone. If I can help others become good field inspectors, then my day is good. There is nothing more fulfilling than helping people reach their goals. That might be my pastor's heart talking.

This is not a complete guide to Mastering Mortgage Field Inspections, but it is here to give you some information that is not usually shared before considering this as a career or a side gig. I thought it was important to explain why field inspectors are essential to a healthy housing market and the different types of inspections. I gave you a list of tools that I used while in the field.

We also discussed on-site inspections and the challenges and difficult situations that can arise.

Since cell phones have come into existence, it has streamlined the inspection process. Inspectors can complete numerous inspections in one day, opposed to just a few. Reporting is done inside mobile apps today and submitted on site. It is also important to keep up with industry standards and changes and to continue to learn your craft.

Time is valuable, and if you took time from your life to read my book, I am grateful to you.

If you enjoyed the book or were able to learn or benefit from it, please leave me a favorable review on Amazon. It would be much appreciated.